I, COFFEE AND THE MOON

CHARU KALDANTE

To,

The Moon, coffee

And the one!

Contents

She Talks To The Moon

The Stunning Piece Of Art

The Golden Hour

Keep Going

Present Moment

Missing Piece

A Beautiful Day To Dream

What If

A Sunset

I'll Be Good To You

A Story Of A Selfie

A Rainy Day

A Rainbow

My Colour Palette

You Will Be In My Prayer

He

I Talk To The Moon

Standing By The Beach

She Is The One!

The Girl In Me Loves The Woman I Am Becoming!

She talks to the moon

She talks to the moon:

About her struggles, her aspirations,

Her insecurities, her desires.

The Moon could see

The bewildering twinkle in her eyes

While she talks,

And how gracious she looks

When she walks.

The Moon knows

She is emotional yet strong,

She accepts her mistakes wholeheartedly

When she is wrong.

How passionate she is about her dreams,

And the heart that has been filled and emptied too soon she carries.

She believes in the Universe,

For its magical energy and the cosmic arrangements,

That is why she holds onto the things little longer only to see their perfect alignments.

On the darkest days, she turns to an artist and a dreamer to escape the reality,

The little did she know

The Moon has already started falling in love with this mystery!

The stunning piece of art

She has beautiful eyes full of hopes and dreams

She speaks with wild passion, her heart that carries

Her eyes are windows to the soul

What they hold is more valuable than gold

They see the colours you haven't seen

They capture the places you haven't been

They talk a lot of hidden emotions and mystery

That emerge from inside and become a beautiful poetry

A cup of coffee in hand, twinkle in her eyes and love in heart

If you stare at her, you will see the stunning piece of art!

The golden hour

The golden hour,

Staring outside the window

She reflects on the day and ultimately on her life.

Her heart feels heavy

The journey seems to be too long to see the light at the end of the tunnel.

The air is full of nothingness and darkness

Even the slightest discomfort may break her down.

For when she looks at the sun that's staring back at her broken soul

She knows that

The little life is still left to cheer her up.

And the dreams are still flowing through her veins.

She cries one more time only to feel happy at the end of the day.

Standing in front of the setting sun

She knows that the light within her still refuses to set!

Keep going

Keep going

Not because it is inevitable

But the life has so much to offer.

Embrace the change

Express gratitude

Make the inner journey

The realm of darkness and light

For the life

Unlived adventures

Of untold stories

That awaits you

There is life

Beyond grief, hurt,

Unanswered questions

For the uncertainty

A wild field of new opportunities

Are welcoming you

With open arms.

Know that

Your dreamy fairy tale

You are chosen to meet,

As the universe skips

A heart beat!

Present moment

It takes a while to live in the present moment,

Either you constantly dwell in the past

Or you get anxious thinking about the future

After a while you start learning to keep a balance between holding on and letting go,

You begin to heal and accept your defeats,

With the grace of a woman, not the grief of the child

One day you wake up and your heart doesn't ache thinking about the past,

You start making plans to make the future beautiful by taking actions in the present

You plant your own garden and decorate your own soul

Without waiting for someone else to buy you flowers

You learn that you really are resilient

You really do have worth

You really are strong and break the fence,

You learn and learn

With every goodbye you learn

And you learn to live in the present tense!

Missing piece

Do you ever just sit down all by yourself

Thinking about that one missing piece?

You search for it everywhere,

Every corner of the world,

Into the uncertain unknown.

For your heart knows

Once you look inside

And there it is,

That one missing piece

And you become the whole!

A beautiful day to dream

It's a beautiful day to dream

With your eyes closed or wide open

To smell the flowers in your garden

Share a smile with a stranger on road

Watch tiny fishes playing in fish tank

See yourself being successful with the feet on ground but still above all

Experience the unknown

Struggle through the challenges and come out of hard times

Later laugh at your old version and reminisce the old memories.

Say goodbye to people with tears in your eyes

And promise to meet them soon on the other side

Leave the comfort zone and travel the world

Make paper planes with the kids in your neighbourhood

Get on those planes and catch the butterflies

Only to come back home with another dream in your eyes.

Again it's a beautiful day to dream

And achieve great heights!!

What if

What if the plan is cancelled, make another plan;

Don't be nervous baby, be happy if you can!

Everything happens for a reason, just trust the God,

He must be right, even if it is odd.

Pick up the book, drink hot coffee,

Get the beauty sleep and eat that toffee.

Change the destination, search for new places,

Pack your bags and put on sunglasses.

Live every moment and do not keep cribbing,

Life is a vacation, enjoy it chilling!!

A sunset

A sunset,

Room full of coffee aroma,

I, standing in the balcony,

Cup of coffee in one hand ,

Few thoughts brewing in mind,

Orange sky being my canvas,

On which I freely etch all my emotions!

I'll be good to you

I am not good at lot of things

I can't paint the pictures

Because the beautiful things witnessed by my eyes

Can't be translated.

I can't sing

As my voice shakes

Out of nowhere

I can't dance

I am too shy

To look at you, watching me

I can't control my tears

I feel too much

Too deep

But I can caress your hair

When your day becomes

Too much to bear

I am not good at much

But I'll be good to you!

A story of a selfie

We took a selfie,

You gave it a caption signing your name on it,

I saved it in the gallery as my favourite,

Hoping to see you again!

Little did I know

That the Universe was watching over us.

The Universe has already started making the plans to reunite us.

Till then that picture will remain my favourite and I'll keep reminiscing the moment!

A rainy day

Sometimes when it rains, I think about you. I think about what you would be doing this very moment. I think about our "rainy" dates at our places. How I used to get afraid of lightning and how you used to take me in your arms and comfort me.

I think about the text when you once said, you would want to dance with me in the rain on the terrace. And I think about how long it would actually take for this thing to happen.

Sometimes when it's raining here, I wonder if it's raining where you are too!

A rainbow

"Did I matter to you today?"

Rainbow asked her.

"Of course!

You reminded me of him!"

"Colorful and cheerful"

My colour palette

Here.

Everyday.

The sky becomes my canvas.

Will you be the color palette to my beautiful sky?

You will be in my prayer

I can be myself, when I am with you

Meet me once and my day will never be blue

No fear of being judged, no fake thoughts

Whatever I speak, it directly comes from the heart

I can con conquer the world, when you are with me

Believe in my wings and I will fly free

Climb the ladder of success, together we are a team

I promise to be with you to fulfil your life's dream

I am very fortunate, because such relations are rare

One thing you should know, you will always be in my prayer!!

He

They might be beverages,

But he is the morning coffee

They might be colours,

But he is the rainbow

They might be highway roads,

But he is the road covered with trees

They might be latest Bollywood songs,

But he is the soothing instrumental music

They might be stars,

But he is the Sun

They might be best friends,

But he is the Soulmate!

I talk to the moon

I talk to the moon!

I talk to the moon-

How vulnerable I become these days

How I struggle to be strong

How people still call me brave and courageous

For staying all by myself

How I try to give my best

How I work hard to fulfil my dreams

Though I fail many times

How I deal with my battles

How I wear my heart on my sleeve

And meanwhile,

How I miss being with you

I talk to the moon-

How you encourage me

How you make me smile from distance

How you make me feel about myself

How mischievous you are

How cold hearted you look

But deep down

I know

You care for me

How your words cheer me up

When I breakdown

How much grateful I am

For having you in my life!

I talk to the moon-

About me

About you

About 'us'

Anything and everything

I talk to the moon!

Standing by the beach

Standing by the beach,

She whispers into his ears-

I am the ocean in the Universe

And you be my shore.

Always there for me

Being strong by my side

Supporting me

And I'll always love you

As deep as the ocean!!

She is the one!

She will be an ice, she will be fire

All her things you will admire

She will be calm just like a river

If you mess with her, she will forgive you never

Her emotions will be deep just like a sea

Dare you play with them, you will pay the fee

She will love you unconditionally, pour her heart out

Give her priority, your attention and you will be proud

She is the one, better if you soon realize

Once she is gone, you will regret it the whole life!

The girl in me loves the woman I am becoming!

The girl in me loves the woman I am becoming!

The girl in me thinks, I could have done much better in life.

The woman in me thinks, "If I could have; I would have!"

The girl in me hates being so emotional.

The woman feels the emotions and let them go.

She cries, washes her face, drinks coffee and is ready to rock the world as if nothing has happened.

The girl used to think, "Why me?"

The woman thinks, "Oh again? Try me!"

The girl didn't give up on the way and the woman is getting stronger day by day.

The girl in me loves the woman I am becoming,

And the woman I am becoming is proud of the girl in me!

www.ingramcontent.com/pod-product-compliance
Lightning Source LLC
Chambersburg PA
CBHW021146130726
47988CB00004B/1493